Captain Patty's

WISDOM HACKS

More Books by Patty Bear

From Plain to Plane:
My Mennonite Childhood, a National Scandal,
and an Unconventional Soar to Freedom

House of the Sun:
A Visionary Guide for Parenting in a Complex World

Unmasking Patriarchy:
Emotional Maturity as a Revolutionary Path

(Coming November 2025 – Available for preorder)

Captain Patty's

WISDOM HACKS

*20 Tools for Clarity,
Direction, and
Self-Leadership*

PATTY BEAR

BARNSTORMERS PRESS

Published in 2025 by
Barnstormers Press

Hardcover ISBN: 978-0-9975735-9-6
E-ISBN: 979-8-9994659-0-0

Interior design by Stacey Aaronson

Printed in the United States of America

For those who long to navigate life with intention, clarity, and quiet courage—and for those who dare to dream, take on hard things, and live with fierce integrity. May these pages meet you at a turning point and help you find your way forward. Not with a map— but with a compass.

Contents

Captain Patty's

WISDOM HACKS

CULTIVATING WISDOM

Age is no guarantee of wisdom.

Plenty of people grow older without growing wiser. That's not a criticism—it's just a truth. Because wisdom isn't something we drift into. It's a place we choose to move toward. A state we practice. A way of seeing, sensing, and responding to life that must be cultivated on purpose.

Wisdom is alive.

It isn't just something we read about or admire from a distance—it's something we live into. It deepens over time, but only if we engage it. It ripens in us when we're willing to face hard truths, take full responsibility for our own clarity, and practice applying insight to reality—especially when it's uncomfortable.

Some of life's hardest lessons aren't optional.

They're part of how our soul gets forged. And no quote or clever phrase can replace the slow, sacred work of metabolizing those experiences. But wisdom doesn't have to come *only* through hardship. That's the myth. Like practicing maneuvers and emergencies in a simulator, what we cultivate now—how we prepare, reflect, and practice discernment—builds skill and strengthens our capacity to respond not just react under pressure. It equips us to meet future difficulty with grace, competence, and confidence.

This book offers 20 tools for cultivating your own living wisdom.

They're simple, but not shallow. You may find yourself returning to them again and again—adapting them, testing them, making them your own. That's the point. Use these entries like you would a compass, a weather check, or a gouge before a checkride: not as a script, but as a way of orienting yourself more clearly.

Because the path to wisdom isn't paved.

It's navigated.

LIKE IT OR LOVE IT?

Wisdom is not just knowing what you want.
It's knowing what's true for you—and worth the cost.

The Story Behind the Hack

When my daughter was around eight or ten, we had regular standoffs in dressing rooms. She wanted everything. I had a budget—and a history. I'd been through my own painful lessons of spending money on things I *had* to have, only to find them months later in the closet, unworn. What had seemed like a need was actually just a hit of desire, followed by the slow shame spiral of spending regret.

Eventually, I knew I had to do something different.

At the time, I devised a strange but effective hack. When catalogues came in the mail, I'd grab a black marker and let myself circle everything I wanted. No guilt. No filters. Just permission to name the wanting. Then I'd close the catalogue and promise myself not to act on anything for a few days. When I returned later and looked again—with the prices and timing and usefulness in mind—most of the urgency had evaporated. Clarity had arrived.

What I thought I loved was often just a like. And when I set those likes aside, what I truly loved became more visible—and more satisfying to say yes to.

So one day, while my daughter and I were in yet another store arguing about another stack of must-haves, it hit me. I said, "Here's the deal. If you really *love* something, I'll get it for you. But if you just *like* it, let's set it aside. Let's trust that what you really love will show up in another store—or another moment."

She paused. Thought about it. Then started saying, "I like this, but I don't love it." And sure enough, in the next store, she found something she *did* love. No fights. No regrets. That tool became a family compass—and she (and I) still uses it today.

How to Use This Tool

"Like it or love it?" is a quick-access clarity check—but it's backed by deep discernment. It's not just about preferences. It's about energetic alignment, real value, and long-term peace.

You can use this tool for purchases, yes. But also for:

+ Choosing a college or job
+ Deciding whether to attend an event
+ Evaluating relationships, invitations, or creative opportunities
+ Determining if something is truly worth the investment—*financially, emotionally, energetically*

But don't skip the inner math.

The Inner Math

Loving something doesn't mean ignoring its cost.

Love includes awareness. If that dream house you adore would cause you financial strain every single month, that strain might change how "love" actually feels in your body. If that relationship is exciting and a lot of fun but the person is immature, that cost is going to become quite expensive in a long-term relationship. If the job sounds prestigious and well-paid, but the schedule would drain your energy, keep you away from your family, or cost you your health, the "love" for that role might not hold up under the weight of your real values.

Sometimes what we think we love is too expensive to be wise. Other times, it's so right that we're willing to pay the price. Either way, the goal is alignment—not illusion.

Discernment grows with practice. At first, you might not be able to feel the difference between like and love right away. That's okay. Give it time. Start small. Pay attention to the feeling in your body. Peace is your north star.

When you get it right, there's no second-guessing. No "shoulda, coulda, woulda." No FOMO. Just clarity.

The Vibe To Look For

"I like it." → Mild enthusiasm. Feels fleeting. Awareness of stress comes up or of crowding out a better choice. You can walk away.

"I love it." → Clear, calm knowing. Feels solid in the body. You're at peace with the cost.

✧ ✧ ✧

Discernment is a muscle.

"Like it or love it" is how you strengthen it.

✧ ✧ ✧

A conversation with yourself
(or with an Anam Cara)

1. What part of my current life feels most connected to this hack?

2. Was there a season in my past where this tool would have made a difference?

3. Where in my life could applying this tool shake up the status quo?

4. Who do I see who lives this wisdom—or could use it now?

5. Who might enjoy exploring the possibilities of this hack with me?

✧ ✧ ✧

Want company on the journey?

You're invited to The Flying Club Lounge on Facebook—a space to engage, exchange ideas, and explore how these tools come to life in real conversations.
Where growth is the adventure—
and you don't have to do it alone.

Find us here:

https://bit.ly/TheFlyingClubLounge

THe GrounD DOeSn'T Care

Reality isn't cruel. It's just not sentimental.
It doesn't wait for your healing before it delivers consequences.

The Story Behind
The Hack

This wisdom was forged in the cockpit.

I can't pinpoint the moment it crossed over from aviation into my inner world, but the seeds were planted early—at the U.S. Air Force Academy—when I first heard one of our five permitted responses as cadets:

"No excuse, sir/ma'am."

At the time, I found it mildly outrageous. I believed, reasonably, that life had exceptions. That sometimes there *were* good reasons. And of course, in human terms, that's true.

There's room for compassion, trauma, and complexity. But aviation isn't built on compassion. It's built on physics.

And the ground?

The ground doesn't care.

In high-performance aircraft, a moment's lapse, a misjudged angle, a missed call—it doesn't matter why. The ground makes no moral calculations. There are no do-overs. Cause and effect *is* the law. And when you fly, that law becomes a daily meditation. You can have a bad day. Your heart can be broken. But the ground is still there, waiting. You either re-spect it—or hit it.

I remember the weight of this more acutely the day I passed my checkride and flew as an airline captain for the first time. Several hundred souls behind me had entrusted their lives to my leadership. Their families would live with the consequences of *my* decisions. I had no room for excuses. Only responsibility.

Of course, pilots are human. So are doctors. So are military leaders. So are parents. We all carry stress. We all carry wounds. But the Law of Gravity doesn't care.

"Your spouse is leaving you?" The ground doesn't care.

"You had a terrible childhood?" The ground doesn't care.

"You're feeling stung by criticism?" The ground doesn't care.

"They're not treating you fairly?" The ground doesn't care.

"You don't like your job, your boss, your pay?" The ground. Does. Not care.

Because consequences don't wait until you feel ready. And some choices—or failures to choose—come with permanent costs.

This isn't about cruelty. This is about respect.

Respect for reality. Respect for responsibility. Respect for the fact that life itself is not engineered around your feelings, your trauma, or your ego. You can—and must—heal. But you still need to show up for what's real.

How To Use This Tool

"The ground doesn't care" isn't a weapon. It's a wake-up call.

It's what you use when you're slipping into excuses.

When you know something needs to change and you're waiting to feel better before you act.

When you're tempted to treat reality like it should pause and wait for your readiness.

Use this tool when:

+ You need to make a hard choice, and your emotions are clouding the facts
+ You're tempted to avoid responsibility because you're overwhelmed or hurt
+ You're hoping that intentions will somehow outweigh actions
+ You need to re-anchor yourself in what's *real* —not just what's *fair*

This tool will *not* replace compassion. But it will prevent collapse.

The Inner Math

Life offers grace—but not immunity.

It's possible to honor your pain, history, or disadvantages and still say:

What are my choices right now? What's the reality? What must I do, regardless of how I feel?

The Law of Gravity is the Law of Cause and Effect. It doesn't respond to mood, motive, or fairness. It responds to trajectory, momentum, structure, discipline.

That's why it's such a powerful internal compass.

Not to shame you—but to call forth your best.

The Vibe To Look For

"This isn't fair." → Valid emotion. But reality still needs action.

"This is hard." → True. And it still must be done.

"I'm not ready." → Then adjust your speed, but don't abdicate responsibility.

"This hurts." → Yes. Honor it. *And do what reality requires.*

✧ ✧ ✧

The ground doesn't care.

And if you learn to respect it, you'll earn the right to fly.

✧ ✧ ✧

A conversation with yourself
(or with an Anam Cara)

1. What part of my current life feels most connected to this hack?

2. Was there a season in my past where this tool would have made a difference?

3. Where in my life could applying this tool shake up the status quo?

4. Who do I see who lives this wisdom—or could use it now?

5. Who might enjoy exploring the possibilities of this hack with me?

✧ ✧ ✧

DREAMING IS FREE

You don't have to pay for possibility.
You only have to open the door.
Let it in. Let it play. Let it show you what wants to live.

The Story Behind the Hack

This one came naturally to me. I never had to learn it—I just lived it.

As a child growing up on a potato farm, tucked far back from the road, I spent hours roaming fields and meadows with a freedom that didn't exist in the rest of my life. I was raised in an Old Order Mennonite community—a world bound by rules, both spoken and silent. But no one could police my imagination.

While the outer world was small and strict, my inner world was vast. Books and magazines opened doorways. The contrails of airplanes scrawled freedom across the sky.

And in my mind, I wandered. I dreamed.

When life got hard, I imagined different futures. I tried on possible lives like outfits in a dressing room. Maybe I'd be a doctor. (Until I tried to dissect a worm and dry heaved.)

Maybe I'd be an architect. (Until I discovered I couldn't draw a straight line.)

I tried on versions of myself and put them back. And it all felt so normal . . . until I realized that not everyone dreams.

Some people are afraid to dream because they're afraid to be *wrong*. Others are afraid to dream because they're tired of being *disappointed*. Still others don't dream because they can't yet see how what they want could ever be possible. And some have simply decided dreaming is childish—or dangerous.

But here's what I know for sure: Dreaming is the headwater of everything good.

Without dreaming, we can't build.

Without dreaming, we can't act.

Without dreaming, we only react—forever focused

on what we *don't* want, and never getting around to discovering what we *do*.

How to Use This Tool

Dreaming is not the same as action. It's what comes *before* action. And if you skip this stage, you skip the clarity that makes action meaningful.

Let yourself try on possibilities like clothing in a dressing room. No obligation. No commitment. No need to explain. Just imagine:

- ✦ What if?
- ✦ What could be?
- ✦ If anything were possible, what would I choose—and why?

You don't owe anyone an answer. You don't have to know how it will happen. You don't have to choose between what you want and what you can afford.

Just *dream.* Because dreaming is free.

The Inner Math

Most of what you dream will never materialize—and it's not supposed to. Your dreams are compost, blueprints, tuning forks, brushstrokes. They are the *raw material* from which clarity emerges.

The more you dream, the more clearly you'll feel the shape of what really matters. The signal gets stronger. Your sense of direction sharpens. Action becomes easier—because you're not guessing anymore.

But first, you have to generate *quantity* before clarity can arise.

Don't worry about alignment yet. Don't worry about the "how." The "how" never shows up until after the commitment. And you can't commit to something you haven't yet imagined.

The Vibe to Look For

Dreaming isn't deciding. *It's wondering.*

Dreaming isn't delusion. *It's opening a portal.*

Dreaming isn't childish. *It's creative research.*

Dreaming isn't expensive.

Dreaming is free.

Let your soul pour. No edits. No budget. No guilt.

Just possibility.

✧ ✧ ✧

A conversation with yourself
(or with an Anam Cara)

1. What part of my current life feels most connected to this hack?

2. Was there a season in my past where this tool would have made a difference?

3. Where in my life could applying this tool shake up the status quo?

4. Who do I see who lives this wisdom—or could use it now?

5. Who might enjoy exploring the possibilities of this hack with me?

✧ ✧ ✧

TINY IS TERRIFIC

Don't wait to feel ready.
Don't wait to know the outcome.
Just take a single, sacred step.
Tiny is not insignificant.
Tiny is how everything begins.

The Story Behind the Hack

I am a master procrastinator. I always have been.

Some of my delays were wise, I now realize. There were times in my life when I wasn't ready—emotionally, energetically, practically—for the opportunity I thought I wanted. And not getting it was grace. Because had I tried too soon, I might've failed, lost heart, and never tried again.

But that's not the kind of procrastination I'm talking about here.

This hack is for the *other* kind.

The kind that comes from fear of failure.

The kind that says, "Don't start unless you're guaranteed a breakthrough."

The kind that waits for perfect clarity, perfect conditions, or a perfect plan before it takes action.

It's the kind of procrastination that doesn't feel restful. It feels painful. Haunted. Stuck.

And here's what I've learned:

Most procrastination isn't about laziness or discipline. It's about uncertainty, fear, and pressure.

"Tiny is Terrific" is the tool I use when I feel paralyzed.

It says:

I don't know what life has in store for me. But I'm going to move. Some direction. Some skill. Some step. And I'm going to make it *tiny*. On purpose.

How to Use This Tool

The key to "Tiny is Terrific" is that you *don't* aim for progress.

You don't aim for momentum. You don't aim for results. You aim for movement. That's it.

- ✦ Don't know what your purpose is? Read one article.
- ✦ Can't make yourself go to the gym? Put on your shoes and stand outside.
- ✦ Avoiding a financial mess? Open one envelope.
- ✦ Dreaming about a creative life? Write one sentence. Paint one color.
- ✦ Want to change your life? Make one tiny decision differently than you would yesterday.

I used to tell clients that if you saved just one penny a day, that mattered.

Not because the penny was enough—but because you were shifting your identity.

From passive to engaged. From paralyzed to present.

The Inner Math

Tiny bypasses perfectionism. Tiny slips past the fear that says, "This has to matter." Tiny removes the pressure of needing to know what comes next.

Tiny builds trust. And trust builds momentum.

When you commit to small movement, you might find yourself saying:

"Oh, that wasn't so bad. Maybe I'll go a little further."

Or not. And that's okay. You still moved. That's all you're ever responsible for: the next honest inch.

The Vibe to Look For

"This won't make a difference." → That's the lie procrastination tells.

"It has to be big to be real." → Another lie. Tiny is the seed of all things.

"But I don't know what I'm doing." → Doesn't matter. Just show up. Tiny doesn't ask you to know. It asks you to begin.

✧ ✧ ✧

You don't have to know where you're going.

Just start walking.

Tiny is movement.

And movement is everything.

✧ ✧ ✧

A CONVERSATION WITH YOURSELF
(or with an Anam Cara)

1. What part of my current life feels most connected to this hack?

2. Was there a season in my past where this tool would have made a difference?

3. Where in my life could applying this tool shake up the status quo?

4. Who do I see who lives this wisdom—or could use it now?

5. Who might enjoy exploring the possibilities of this hack with me?

✧ ✧ ✧

YOUR HABITS ARE YOUR WEALTH

Real wealth isn't what you can count.
It's what you can count on.
Especially when things fall apart.

The Story Behind
the Hack

The mark of a wisdom hack is its universality. It applies across seasons—inner and outer.

This one came from my love of gardening.

In garden design, you start with the *bones* of the garden. In winter—when flowers fade and leaves fall—what remains? If the structure is sound, it still holds beauty. Integrity is visible even in dormancy.

If it has good bones, it will be gorgeous in the dead of winter.

But this hack didn't stay poetic. It came crashing into my personal and professional life.

Loss can be disorienting. So can success. And when things are going unexpectedly well, there's often a fear just beneath the surface:

What if it all crashes?

What if the customers stop coming?

What if someone gets sick?

What if the rug gets pulled out from under me?

For me, those "what ifs" became real after 9/11.

My airline was one of the two that lost planes, crews, and passengers. My husband lost his job. Our companies filed for bankruptcy. I feared I would lose my job too.

We had two children, one income, and a lot of uncertainty. We lost our pensions. Our salaries were cut in half. In the airline industry, what followed became known as *the lost decade*.

Others had it worse, of course—many lost loved ones or were sent off to war. But for me, that season became intensely clarifying. It showed me not just what I had to lose—but what I could still rely on.

I'd grown up on a farm where money was scarce. I knew how to work hard—really hard. I knew how to be frugal. How to make things stretch.

And while I didn't want to go back to that kind of striving, I knew I could. And that gave me something more valuable than money: I had proof that I carried wealth inside me. Not just traits. Habits.

Habits of work, resilience, thrift, discipline, and clarity.

That realization became a lifelong anchor: Your habits are your wealth.

How to Use This Tool

Most people think of wealth in terms of money—because that's what's measurable. But money is just one expression of value.

True wealth includes:

+ The skills you've built
+ The mindsets you've trained
+ The character you've cultivated
+ The relationships you've nurtured
+ The habits no one can take from you

Take inventory of what's already in your internal "wealth account":

- ✦ Maybe you communicate clearly

- ✦ Maybe you read emotional energy well

- ✦ Maybe you're organized, resourceful, or self-aware

- ✦ Maybe you keep showing up even when you're scared

- ✦ Maybe you've trained yourself to think critically, recover quickly, or see what others miss

These aren't just strengths. They're cultivated patterns. They're habits. And they're *yours*.

The Inner Math

When everything external feels unstable, your habits are the stability that travels with you.

They're the muscle memory of your values. They're your invisible infrastructure.

Even the smallest, most ordinary habit—saving a dollar, pausing before reacting, finishing what you start—builds something real.

And the beauty is: You don't need to already have all the habits you want. You can start investing today:

- ✦ Want to feel calmer? Build the habit of pausing to respond rather than react.
- ✦ Want to improve your communication? Take a breath before speaking.
- ✦ Want to feel more confident? Build the habit of completing small promises.
- ✦ Want to feel more free? Build the habit of telling the truth—to yourself.

Every habit you build is a deposit into your future resilience.

The Vibe To Look For

"What if I lose everything?" → Then ask, *what will still be mine?*

"What if things collapse?" → Then fall back on your foundation.

"What if the numbers aren't enough?" → Then trust your internal account.

✧ ✧ ✧

If you've built solid habits, you'll always be richer than your bank account. Because that's the kind of wealth no crisis can wipe out.

A CONVERSATION WITH YOURSELF
(or with an Anam Cara)

1. What part of my current life feels most connected to this hack?

2. Was there a season in my past where this tool would have made a difference?

3. Where in my life could applying this tool shake up the status quo?

4. Who do I see who lives this wisdom—or could use it now?

5. Who might enjoy exploring the possibilities of this hack with me?

✧ ✧ ✧

Leave Your Neighborhood

At some point, life will ask you to go
where no one knows you—
so you can finally meet yourself.

The Story Behind
the Hack

I got on an airplane by myself at eighteen to begin a new chapter of my life at the U.S. Air Force Academy.

I'd never visited before saying yes to the four-year commitment—and the seven-year commitment that would follow. I couldn't afford to visit first.

I was terribly homesick. But underneath the ache was a secret relief.

For the first time, I was going somewhere no one knew my story. No one connected me to the Plain People dresses and bonnets of my upbringing. No one linked me to the swirl of religious and family scandal that had landed my community in the pages of national newspapers.

Here, I didn't stand out for what my mother wore. I didn't carry the weight of my family's past. I could forge my own identity—for better or worse.

And that was the beginning. Not just of a new place. But a new self.

Your "neighborhood" is your comfort zone. It's the terrain you know. The people who know you—or at least the version of you they've grown used to.

You may love your neighborhood. You may hate it. But you know what to expect. And it knows what to expect from you.

There comes a moment in every adult's life—sometimes subtle, sometimes seismic—when you're invited to leave that familiar ground. Sometimes, as it was for me, the leaving is literal. Other times, it's internal.

But in every case, it's a crossing. A psychological, emotional, or spiritual threshold. Not a rebellion against others—but a rebellion against your *younger self*:

The small, dependent, unquestioned version of you that developed in a closed system.

Leaving your neighborhood is how you claim your adulthood. It's how you step into the open field of who you're becoming—even when no one else recognizes you yet.

How to Use This Tool

Every stage of life comes with a developmental task. And here's the hard part: there's no deadline, no external enforcement. You can avoid the task and *nothing will happen right away.* No one will call you out. You're an adult. It's your choice.

But down the road, life circles back to test your growth. If you've refused the task, you'll feel it in sharp relief. What once seemed intimidating now looms like a mountain. You can still cross it, but the cost—and consequences—are higher now.

One of those critical tasks is this:

Leave your neighborhood.

Go where no one knows you.

Go where the familiar projections don't follow.

Go where you're not "the funny one," or "the quiet one," or "the responsible one."

Go where no one holds the history of your childhood mistakes.

Go where your voice, your values, and your contribution must stand on their own.

This is how you find out who you are *without the echo of your upbringing*.

The Inner Math

You don't have to cut ties with your friends, your family, or your literal neighbors. But you do need to know—deep in your bones—that you can stand on your own.

This is about self-sufficiency and sovereignty.

It means cultivating the ability to survive—not just financially, but emotionally, intellectually, relationally, and spiritually—from what you *generate within yourself*.

It's about finding your footing on new ground. And discovering that you are capable of walking it.

There's a kind of confidence that *only* comes from this passage. And it can't be given. It must be earned.

The Vibe To Look For

"I'm not unhappy where I am." → That doesn't mean you've grown all you can.

"I don't want to disappoint anyone." → This isn't about them. It's about your evolution.

"But what if I don't know who I am without them?" → That's exactly the point.

◇ ◇ ◇

Go where no one knows you. Let your identity reintroduce itself.

Leaving your neighborhood isn't abandonment. It's arrival.

It's how you claim the life your younger self couldn't yet imagine.

A conversation with yourself
(or with an Anam Cara)

1. What part of my current life feels most connected to this hack?

2. Was there a season in my past where this tool would have made a difference?

3. Where in my life could applying this tool shake up the status quo?

4. Who do I see who lives this wisdom—or could use it now?

5. Who might enjoy exploring the possibilities of this hack with me?

✧ ✧ ✧

BE A LOVER
OF REALITY

Reality isn't unkind.
It just doesn't bend to protect our illusions.
And when you stop asking it to—
you get your freedom back.

The Story Behind
the Hack

There came a point in my life when I had to stop asking someone to be who I wished they were. Not because they were terrible. But because my peace was too important to keep bargaining away.

I had tried. I'd left the door open—more than once. I'd set the stage for repair, hoped for insight, crafted careful invitations for change.

But the turning point came quietly, as turning points often do.

I realized: *This is who they are.*

Not evil. Not incapable of love. Just unwilling—or unable—to go deeper. And the only question left was: *How do I live with that in practical terms?*

It wasn't just about accepting others. Sometimes, the person I had to stop bargaining with . . . was me.

There were seasons when *I* was the one unable to rise to the challenge. When I wasn't ready to face the full truth. When I avoided, excused, delayed—because reality felt too sharp to touch.

But when I finally chose to love reality—not excuse it, not collapse under it, but truly accept it—I felt a strange and holy kind of freedom.

It didn't come with trumpets. But it came with peace.

Life can be beautiful—and it can be brutal. Sometimes we try to cushion ourselves from reality's sharp edges.

We soften the truth with substances.

We bury ourselves in busyness.

We take shelter in denial or hope or wishful thinking.

We tell ourselves:

"He didn't really mean that."

"She had good intentions."

"It's not that bad."

"I don't really need anything."

"I'm fine."

And sometimes . . . that's okay.

Sometimes we *do* need to rest on those cushions until we're ready—until we've gathered enough strength to really see.

But eventually, life calls us out of the fog and says:

Come witness what's real. Without excuses. Without delay. Not to punish you. But to *free you.*

How To Use This Tool

To be a lover of reality doesn't mean you stop dreaming. It means you stop gaslighting yourself.

You start to notice things like:

- ✦ The early signs that something's off
- ✦ The mismatch between words and actions
- ✦ The character gaps that keep repeating

+ The systems, people, or patterns that drain or distort

And instead of rationalizing or minimizing, you say:

"I see that."

"That happened."

"This is what's true right now."

You don't have to take action yet. You don't have to fix anything or confront anyone. You just have to witness it. Fully. Without flinching. That's the first movement toward wisdom.

The Inner Math

Reality always has a cost. That's part of what makes it real.

When we ignore what's true early—

+ In the first red flag of a relationship
+ In the early sprout of a lie
+ In the first crack in someone's character

We don't escape the price. We *increase* it. What we avoid in the beginning eventually demands everything.

So love reality when it's small. Catch the pattern while it's still soft.

Don't wait until it's wrapped around your life and requires a crowbar to extract.

Being a lover of reality isn't about judgment or harshness. It's about devotion to *what is*.

The Vibe To Look For

"I don't want to believe this." → That's okay. Just witness it.

"Maybe it'll get better." → Maybe. But first, get honest about what *is*.

"I don't want to hurt anyone." → Seeing clearly isn't violence. It's preparation.

"But I love them." → Good. Then let that love include the truth.

✧ ✧ ✧

Being a lover of reality means letting truth come all the way in—without resistance, without editing, without apology.

It's not cruelty. It's clarity. And clarity is love.

A conversation with yourself
(or with an Anam Cara)

1. What part of my current life feels most connected to this hack?

2. Was there a season in my past where this tool would have made a difference?

3. Where in my life could applying this tool shake up the status quo?

4. Who do I see who lives this wisdom—or could use it now?

5. Who might enjoy exploring the possibilities of this hack with me?

✧ ✧ ✧

mentor yourself

It's wise to seek counsel.
But it's wiser still
to become someone you trust.

The Story Behind the Hack

Long before I had the language for it, I had an inner presence I could turn to.

As a child, I sometimes thought of it as a "tutor"—a Spirit Guide that could see further than I could, especially in moments of fear or confusion.

It wasn't harsh. It wasn't punishing.

It was steady, wise, and kind.

A companion voice that helped me understand things and see something larger.

Years later, I saw the same thing in my daughter.

She once told me about a moment when she was furious—at her brother, at both her parents—and then suddenly paused and said to herself, *Wait . . . maybe I'm the common denominator here.*

Other times, I'd hear her describe this inner voice as saying things like:

That thing you just did? That's not really who you want to be. Let's do better next time.

It wasn't shaming. It wasn't performative. It was her inner mentor: clear-eyed, kind, and committed to her growth. That's when I realized:

The voice of mentorship doesn't have to come from the outside. It can be cultivated within. And when you learn to recognize it—when you grow it, trust it, and practice returning to it—you become someone you can count on.

We all need mentors at times—people who have walked the path, who can see what we can't, who aren't afraid to say what needs to be said.

But don't stop there. At some point, you have to stop looking *only* outward and start developing the most enduring mentor you'll ever have: the one inside you.

That inner mentor isn't a judge or a critic. It's the part of you that sees clearly. Speaks truthfully. And wants what's best for you—not just what's easiest or most comfortable.

How To Use This Tool

Mentoring yourself means telling yourself the truth—even when it's hard.

Not with self-condemnation.

With *self-honesty*.

It sounds like this:

- ✦ "I made a mistake."
- ✦ "That was my blind spot."
- ✦ "I knew better, but I ignored it."
- ✦ "I gave power to someone who hadn't earned it."

It also sounds like this:

- ✦ "I handled that well."
- ✦ "I've come a long way."
- ✦ "That was wise of me."
- ✦ "I saw that clearly and responded with strength."

Self-mentoring means taking 100 percent responsibility for your results—not for what other people do, but for what *you* chose, tolerated, missed, built, ignored, or pursued. It also means recognizing your gifts—*even when others don't.*

Sometimes the people around you are threatened by your growth. They may downplay your efforts. They may pretend not to notice your excellence. They may subtly encourage you to shrink so they feel safer.

Don't let them define your worth.

Let your inner mentor be your mirror.

The Inner Math

You'll make better decisions when you trust your own discernment. That trust doesn't come from perfection. It comes from *practice.*

Practice being honest with yourself without collapsing.

Practice giving yourself feedback without cruelty.

Practice encouraging yourself without arrogance.

Your inner mentor is the one who says:

"Yes, that could have gone better. Let's learn from it."

"No, you're not crazy. That pattern was real."

"You're ready for more. Let's sharpen the tools."

"You're worth investing in. Let's go."

When you know how to mentor yourself, you'll welcome wise input from others—but you'll never be dependent on it.

The Vibe to Look For

"What did I ignore?" → Ask yourself, kindly.

"What's really true here?" → Sit with it.

"What do I need to develop next?" → Get curious.

"Who gets the final say?" → Let it be the wisest part of *you*.

✧ ✧ ✧

Mentor yourself.

Not because you have all the answers—but because you're committed to living by the clearest ones you can find.

And the clearest ones are almost always inside you, if you're willing to listen.

✧ ✧ ✧

A conversation with yourself
(or with an Anam Cara)

1. What part of my current life feels most connected to this hack?

2. Was there a season in my past where this tool would have made a difference?

3. Where in my life could applying this tool shake up the status quo?

4. Who do I see who lives this wisdom—or could use it now?

5. Who might enjoy exploring the possibilities of this hack with me?

✧ ✧ ✧

POWER IS RESPONSIBILITY

*Power without responsibility is not power.
It's indulgence.
And it always comes at someone else's cost.*

The Story Behind the Hack

I've already shared what it meant to carry the lives of passengers as an airline captain. That was responsibility in its most literal form:

Every decision mattered. When it mattered, the words we spoke in the cockpit carried real consequences.

But power shows up in quieter ways, too—ways that are just as consequential. Sometimes it's financial, emotional, spiritual. Sometimes it's relational—who you affirm, what you tolerate.

And one of the most underestimated forms of power . . . is communication.

Words shape perception. Perception shapes belief. And belief shapes behavior.

That means: Every post. Every endorsement.

Every teaching moment—whether you're leading a team, raising a child, writing a book, or influencing five people on Instagram—has ripple effects.

And we don't get to opt out of those ripples just because we "meant well." We can't control how others hear or misuse our words. But we *can* take responsibility for how they might be weaponized, spiritualized, or used to excuse harmful behavior.

We can speak the truth—without malice, and without enabling immaturity.

We can promote clarity—without cruelty, and without coddling bad actors.

That's 360-degree responsibility. Not just what we say—but what we reinforce.

Not just what we *intend*—but what we *allow*. Because power is not just a platform. It's a sacred trust.

We instinctively know this truth. That's why so many shy away from visibility, from leadership—formal or informal. Because deep down, we know that true power comes with weight.

Responsibility is the cost of power. And when it's carried well, it *builds* power too.

Whether you're leading a team, raising a child, influencing a group, or simply navigating your own life, the truth remains:

The moment you impact others, you are responsible.

How To Use This Tool

Responsibility isn't just a burden. It's a bridge to maturity. A crucible that transforms you.

Start with self-responsibility:

+ Take ownership of your choices, patterns, and outcomes.
+ Stop outsourcing your integrity to what "others are doing."
+ Be someone *you* can trust with power.

Then expand it:

+ If you're a parent, take responsibility for the emotional climate of your home.
+ If you're a leader, take responsibility for the well-being of those who follow you.

- If you hold privilege or status, take responsibility for the impact of your presence and power—even when it's uncomfortable.

And just as importantly: Refuse to be fooled by those who want the perks of power without the price of responsibility.

That's not leadership. That's extraction.

The Inner Math

We've all seen it—people who crave the title, the control, the attention, the perks . . . but who disappear when it's time to take ownership.

This is not strength. It's profound immaturity.

Real power is quiet, steady, and rooted in accountability.

When you embrace responsibility:

- You become strong enough to hold what others can't.
- You become trusted in your community.
- You become capable of building something that lasts.

Responsibility grows capacity. And capacity is the soil where wisdom takes root.

The Vibe To Look For

"I want to be in charge." → Then ask: what weight are you willing to carry?

"They shouldn't get away with that." → Then ask: are *you* showing up accountably? And are you willing to hold them accountable?

"I just want the freedom to do what I want." → Then remember: freedom without responsibility destroys trust—self trust and the trust of others.

✧　✧　✧

Power is not bad.

Accountability is not punishment.

Together, they are the architecture of maturity. They are how we build what matters—and how we keep it standing when storms come.

If you hold any kind of power—formal, relational, social, or spiritual—then this is your charge:

Carry it well.

✧ ✧ ✧

A conversation with yourself
(or with an Anam Cara)

1. What part of my current life feels most connected to this hack?

2. Was there a season in my past where this tool would have made a difference?

3. Where in my life could applying this tool shake up the status quo?

4. Who do I see who lives this wisdom—or could use it now?

5. Who might enjoy exploring the possibilities of this hack with me?

✧ ✧ ✧

REFUSE TO CARRY OTHER PEOPLE'S RESPONSIBILITIES

Embrace responsibility.
But carry only what's yours.
Because carrying what isn't yours doesn't help.
It harms.

The Story Behind the Hack

I've seen this pattern in coaching, in relationships, and in my own reflection. If you relate to this entry it's probably because it's *your* story.

You may not remember when it started. But chances are, you were the one who *noticed* the problem.

Who *understood* what was needed.

Who *stepped in* before anyone asked.

You didn't do it for attention. You did it because someone had to.

This is the universal story of the overly responsible—those forced to grow up too early, those born deeply attuned to others, or those simply wired for resourcefulness, care, and competence.

At first, this can look like compassion. Like maturity. Like leadership. And sometimes it *is*.

Sometimes people truly need help—an illness, a crisis, a season of fragility.

Sometimes someone has to assume command while another gathers strength.

That's not dysfunction. That's community.

But when the season becomes a pattern—

When one person habitually waits, avoids, offloads, or escapes—and another person habitually steps in, takes over, and absorbs the fallout—

That's not kindness.

That's imbalance.

How to Use This Tool

Here's the litmus test:

Are you helping someone through something? Or are you habitually doing for them what they should be learning to do for themselves?

Some people:

+ Wait for others to speak up so they don't risk saying the wrong thing.
+ Let others read their mind so they don't have to name their needs.
+ Shift blame when they behave poorly—and hope you'll absorb it.
+ Withhold effort or clarity until someone else "fills the space" for them.

And if you're highly conscientious, you may step in automatically—without even questioning it.

Don't.

Because here's the truth:

Assuming responsibility that belongs to someone else is not generosity. It's a subtle betrayal of the developmental process.

It robs the other person of the very friction that might have sparked growth.

It creates a false map of accountability—one where the consequences don't land where they should.

We don't take credit for what isn't ours. Let's not take blame or burden that isn't ours either.

The Inner Math

Being responsible for others is different than being responsible to others.

You are responsible to others for your integrity, your clarity, your fairness. But you are not responsible for their emotions, choices, growth, or self-leadership.

When you carry what isn't yours:

- ✦ You exhaust yourself.
- ✦ You enable dependency.
- ✦ You confuse the lines of cause and effect.

Worse—those around you may never develop the muscles they need to carry their own load.

And so the cycle continues.

The Vibe to Look For

"They can't handle it." → Then ask: Are you sure? Or are you just afraid to find out?

"If I don't do it, no one will." → Then let no one do it —and see what happens.

"I just want to be helpful." → Then be helpful in ways that support growth, not avoidance.

✧ ✧ ✧

Love doesn't mean over-functioning.

Compassion doesn't mean no boundaries.

Responsibility is sacred—but only when you're carrying what actually belongs to you.

✧ ✧ ✧

A CONVERSATION WITH YOURSELF
(or with an Anam Cara)

1. What part of my current life feels most connected to this hack?

2. Was there a season in my past where this tool would have made a difference?

3. Where in my life could applying this tool shake up the status quo?

4. Who do I see who lives this wisdom—or could use it now?

5. Who might enjoy exploring the possibilities of this hack with me?

✧ ✧ ✧

DISCOVER WHAT YOU WANT BY NAMING WHAT YOU DON'T

Clarity doesn't always arrive in light.
Sometimes it arrives in irritation.
In friction. In a loud, silent no.
And from that no—a direction.

The Story Behind the Hack

This wisdom was born in a coaching session. Actually— many coaching sessions. Again and again, I worked with clients who were stuck in pain. Some were overwhelmed by a toxic work environment. Others were trapped in patterns of overgiving, stuckness, or chronic confusion.

So I'd ask the obvious question: "What do you want instead?"

And the answer would come back—every time: "I don't know."

No matter how I rephrased it, or how many gentle options I offered, the answer stayed the same. That's when I brought it to my own coach.

She nodded and said, "Sounds like broken wanters."

That phrase stopped me cold. *Broken wanters.* It made perfect sense.

When you've spent years surviving, pleasing, performing, or adapting—when your wants have been ignored, mocked, or punished—your ability to want clearly *atrophies.*

So I started wondering: If you don't know what you want, but you're in acute pain . . .

What if you just start there? What if you stop pretending to feel grateful, and just tell the truth about what's intolerable?

And then I remembered something I'd once read—maybe from Buddhism, maybe from Eastern philosophy—about how the path to healing begins not in transcendence, but in *turning toward your suffering.*

So I tried an experiment. I asked clients to name what they hated. What drained them. What made them ache or bristle or collapse.

And then I asked: "What's the opposite of that?"

"What would relief feel like?"

"If this were the problem . . . what would freedom look like?"

That's when the answers came. Not from affirmation. But from contrast.

That's when I realized: Clarity doesn't always arrive in light. Sometimes it arrives in friction.

We are told to be positive. To focus on gratitude. To look for the light. And yes, there's deep wisdom in that. But sometimes clarity doesn't begin with what's good.

It begins with what's intolerable. It begins when you notice:

+ This doesn't fit.
+ That's not for me.
+ I hate this dynamic.
+ I can't keep living this way.

That kind of negative clarity—when harnessed wisely— is a compass.

How to Use This Tool

There will be times when you cannot yet name what you want. You don't have a model. You've never seen it done. Or you've been so immersed in survival, you haven't even had the luxury to imagine more.

In those moments, don't try to be upbeat. Try to be honest.

Get very, very clear about what you *don't* want:

- ✦ Write a list.
- ✦ Rant on the page.
- ✦ Be petty. Be extreme. Be exact.
- ✦ Circle what makes your shoulders tighten. What drains your joy. What feels like soul-smog.

And then ask: What is the opposite of this? What would feel like relief? Like expansion? Like breath?

That's the beginning of what you want. It may not be fully formed yet—but now you're facing in the right direction.

The Inner Math

Wanting is vulnerable. It implies risk. It opens the door to failure, rejection, disappointment, ridicule.

No wonder so many people stay stuck in what they don't want. Because the moment you name what you *do* want . . . you might have to go for it. And going for it might mean:

- ✦ Leaving the crowd.
- ✦ Becoming visible.
- ✦ Trying something unproven.
- ✦ Becoming the first in your circle to do it differently.

But here's the truth: There is no becoming without wanting. Wanting is not greed. It's growth.

The Vibe To Look For

"I hate this." → Then ask: What would feel like the opposite?

"I don't know what I want." → Then ask: What do I *know* I don't want?

"I'm afraid to want more." → Then ask: What will it cost me if I don't?

✧ ✧ ✧

You don't have to wait for a perfect vision. Start with the friction. Start with what grates. Start with the stone in your shoe. Then turn. Face the direction of relief. Of peace. Of *yes*. And walk.

A conversation with yourself
(or with an Anam Cara)

1. What part of my current life feels most connected to this hack?

2. Was there a season in my past where this tool would have made a difference?

3. Where in my life could applying this tool shake up the status quo?

4. Who do I see who lives this wisdom—or could use it now?

5. Who might enjoy exploring the possibilities of this hack with me?

✧ ✧ ✧

NEW DAY,
NEW JET

Yesterday's mistake doesn't get to fly today's mission.
Unless you let it.

The Story Behind
the Hack

In pilot training, every morning started with a ritual:

Stand-up emergency scenarios. Lights flashing. Sirens wailing. Engine failures.

We'd be grilled on quick-action procedures—evaluating the problem, declaring the emergency, how to get the jet safely back on the ground.

Each new scenario began with a signal from the instructor:

"New day. New jet."

It meant: compartmentalize. Leave the last emergency behind. Start fresh.

I was on one of three critical check rides in the supersonic T-38 when I made an error during aerobatics. I wasn't sure how big a deal it was—only that it was a mistake.

And I was stewing on it—ruminating, replaying, criticizing—while we returned to land.

That's when I made the real error:

I forgot to put the landing gear down before turning final approach.

There *was* still time. But I passed the gear-down limit— a hard safety boundary that, once crossed, meant automatic failure.

I failed that check ride not because of the original mistake. But because I couldn't let it go.

Because I carried the weight of a past moment into a new one—and it cost me.

How To Use This Tool

This hack isn't about denial.

It's not about pretending a mistake didn't happen.

It's about mental discipline.

It's about knowing *when* to debrief.

Mistakes need reflection. But not when you're landing something important.

You can:

- ✦ Own the error.
- ✦ Learn from it.
- ✦ Debrief it with rigor and honesty.

But don't drag it into the next clean slate.

Don't let it poison today's clarity.

Don't let shame override attention.

Don't rehearse failure while you're trying to execute.

If you do . . . you may repeat it.

The Inner Math

There's a quiet lie that shame whispers:

"If I don't keep feeling bad, I won't learn my lesson."

But the opposite is often true.

Clarity teaches. Shame confuses.

Focus corrects. Rumination distorts.

So make a deal with yourself:

When you mess up, take full responsibility.

And when it's time to fly again—New day. New jet.

That means:

+ Let today's challenge be clean.
+ Let your past self be part of your training, not your identity.
+ Let your attention return to the present moment, where performance still lives.

The Vibe to Look For

"I can't believe I did that." → You did. Debrief it. Then move on.

"What if I mess up again?" → Then take what you learned and focus on *this* moment.

"But I haven't earned a fresh start." → You earn it every time you show up with presence, not perfection.

✧ ✧ ✧

Don't contaminate today's flight with yesterday's turbulence.

Learn the lesson. Then leave the shame.

Compartmentalize with care.

Because the mission that matters most is always the one you're flying *right now*.

New day.

New jet.

Cleared for takeoff.

✧ ✧ ✧

A conversation with yourself
(or with an Anam Cara)

1. What part of my current life feels most connected to this hack?

2. Was there a season in my past where this tool would have made a difference?

3. Where in my life could applying this tool shake up the status quo?

4. Who do I see who lives this wisdom—or could use it now?

5. Who might enjoy exploring the possibilities of this hack with me?

✧ ✧ ✧

WHOOP, WHOOP, PULL UP

*There are moments when the only wise move
is to abort the mission and climb.
Fast.*

The Story Behind the Hack

In modern jets, there's a warning system called the Ground Proximity Warning System (GPWS). It's designed to alert pilots when they're dangerously close to the ground—whether because of terrain, distraction, or misjudgment.

The warning is unforgettable:

"WHOOP WHOOP, PULL UP!"

It's loud.

It's jarring.

It's meant to cut through everything else.

At that moment, nothing else matters. Not the checklist. Not the radio. Not the mission.

Just one thing:

Pull up. Now.

No pilot hears this warning in a calm, quiet cockpit. For most, thankfully, the only time they ever hear it is in the simulator.

It always signals overload:

Bad weather. Equipment failures. Distractions. Stress. Too many priorities colliding at once.

Even highly trained pilots can miss signals when the system gets flooded.

And life is no different.

Wouldn't it be nice if we had a Ground Proximity Warning System for *our* lives? Something that blared through the noise when we were too close to emotional or psychological danger?

Sometimes we do:

+ A friend says: "Hey . . . are you okay?"
+ A loved one states a boundary—and then repeats it.

- ✦ Your body starts sounding the alarm through fatigue, illness, panic, or rage.

But more often, the cues are subtle.

We're stressed. Distracted. Numb. And we miss the warning signs.

Until it's too late.

How To Use This Tool

You can't install a mechanical warning system into your life. But you *can* train an internal one.

Start noticing the signs that your system is overloaded:

- ✦ Life feels foggy, frantic, or too quiet.
- ✦ You're pulled in too many directions.
- ✦ You start ignoring gut feelings or physical needs.
- ✦ You feel yourself reacting, shutting down, or spiraling.

That's your moment.

WHOOP WHOOP, PULL UP.

Not analyze.

Not explain.

Not fix.

Just pull back. Away from the ground. Out of the danger zone.

Then—once you're in a clearer, safer place—you can regroup. You can rethink, debrief, and decide what comes next.

Bonus hack:

Designate someone you trust—and give them permission to say *Whoop Whoop, Pull Up* when they see you veering toward danger.

The Inner Math

Life doesn't always offer clear alarms. And when you're overloaded, the first thing to go is discernment.

But danger isn't always explosive. Sometimes it's subtle. Creeping. Eroding your clarity until the crash is inevitable.

This hack gives you a reset point.

A way to say:

"Something's off. I don't know what yet. But I'm not going to crash figuring it out."

That's wisdom.

That's maturity.

That's command presence.

The Vibe To Look For

"I can handle this if I just push a little harder." → Or maybe you're moments from burnout. Pull up.

"It's probably fine." → That's what they say in every accident report. Pull up.

"I can't think straight, but I have to keep going." → No, you don't. Pull up.

✧ ✧ ✧

You don't need to be right. You don't need to fix it all in real time.

You just need to recognize danger—and climb.

Whoop whoop. Pull up.

Live to fly another day.

✧ ✧ ✧

A conversation with yourself
(or with an Anam Cara)

1. What part of my current life feels most connected to this hack?

2. Was there a season in my past where this tool would have made a difference?

3. Where in my life could applying this tool shake up the status quo?

4. Who do I see who lives this wisdom—or could use it now?

5. Who might enjoy exploring the possibilities of this hack with me?

✧ ✧ ✧

EAT YOUR
BOX LUNCH

Emergencies feel urgent.
But reacting without thinking?
That's how good people make things worse.

The Story Behind
The Hack

When I was a brand-new copilot on the KC-135, an instructor gave us a piece of advice I never forgot.

We were running through emergency procedures when he suddenly asked:

"What's the *first* thing you do in an emergency?"

Like trained parrots, a group of us piped up immediately:

"Aviate, navigate, communicate!"

"Fly the jet."

"Execute the boldface."

We were proud of ourselves. Sharp. Precise. Ready.

He shook his head and said:

"No. The first thing you do in an emergency is pull out your box lunch and eat it."

We stared at him. Blank. Bewildered. Was he serious?

And then he explained.

On long flights, we brought along box lunches— simple meals packed in white cardboard boxes. But the advice had nothing to do with sandwiches.

"I don't actually want you to eat," he said. "I want you to *pause*."

In the heat of a crisis, your adrenaline will lie to you. It will convince you that any action is better than no action at all.

But in aviation, a rushed move—like pulling the wrong throttle or stepping on the wrong rudder—can kill you.

The most dangerous action is the wrong one.

And almost every emergency—yes, even in flight— gives you a beat.

A moment to breathe. To center.

To think before you act.

That moment is the difference between a pilot . . . and a panic.

How to Use This Tool

This hack isn't about food. It's about presence under pressure.

The next time something goes sideways—

- ✦ A conversation escalates.
- ✦ A decision feels high-stakes.
- ✦ You're flooded with urgency or fear.

Try this:

Eat your box lunch.

Not literally. But mentally.

Give yourself a beat.

One deep breath.

One quiet question: *What's really happening here?*

That tiny pause can prevent huge damage. And when you truly don't have time to pause—you'll know it.

The Inner Math

Emergencies are part of life. So are perceived emergencies.

Your boss sends a curt email.

Your partner looks disappointed.

A project gets delayed.

Someone criticizes you online.

Your nervous system surges.

Fight-flight takes over.

You want to fix it *now*.

But the urgency you feel may not be real. It might just be a habit.

Or fear.

Or an old trauma script.

This hack breaks the reflex.

It creates room for wisdom to report for duty.

The Vibe To Look For

"I have to say something right now." → Maybe. Or maybe you need a breath.

"If I don't respond immediately, I'll look weak." → Or you'll look wise.

"I feel like I'm under attack." → Eat your box lunch. Regain clarity. Then decide.

✧ ✧ ✧

Fast thinking isn't always smart thinking. And pause is not the same as passivity.

Sometimes the boldest, bravest move you can make is to do nothing for one long breath.

To wait for your wisdom to catch up with your reaction.

To pause long enough to choose the right action—instead of just any action.

Eat your box lunch.

Then handle your emergency.

✧ ✧ ✧

A conversation with yourself
(or with an Anam Cara)

1. What part of my current life feels most connected to this hack?

2. Was there a season in my past where this tool
   would have made a difference?

3. Where in my life could applying this tool shake
   up the status quo?

4. Who do I see who lives this wisdom—or could
   use it now?

5. Who might enjoy exploring the possibilities of
   this hack with me?

✧ ✧ ✧

HOLD YOUR COURSE IN THE CONE OF CONFUSION

Sometimes the smartest move is no move.
Especially when the data goes dark.

The Story Behind
the Hack

Back before GPS made navigation crystal clear, we flew using ground-based radio navigation systems called VORs—short for Very High Frequency Omnidirectional Range.

These stations transmitted 360 directional radials like invisible spokes on a wheel. You'd fly *into* a VOR on one radial, and fly *out* on another—navigating the country, leg by leg.

Far from a VOR, course corrections needed to be big. But as you got closer, the signal became more sensitive. And the closer you got, the smaller your adjustments needed to be—until . . .

You flew right overhead.

And that's when it happened.

The needle on your instrument would start swinging.

From inbound course to outbound course.

From signal strength to signal silence.

You'd be flying in the Cone of Confusion—a zone where your guidance system stopped working.

And the official guidance?

Do nothing.

Hold your course.

Wait for clarity.

In aviation, the Cone of Confusion is a real navigational zone. Right overhead a VOR, your instruments lose lock for a moment.

The signal is shifting from one mode to another, and you don't yet have reliable feedback.

The danger?

If you try to "fix" your course while in the cone—you can make it worse.

The best move is the counterintuitive one:

Do nothing.

Keep flying.

Keep breathing.

Wait for the system to settle.

Let the guidance return.

How to Use This Tool

There are moments in life when your internal guidance system—your instincts, your direction, your clarity—goes fuzzy.

You lose the feeling of certainty. The signal scrambles. And you start to panic.

"I'm off course."

"I've made a mistake."

"I need to do something now."

No, you don't.

You're just in the Cone of Confusion.

And the same advice applies:

Hold your course. Don't make big changes.

Don't react. Don't overcorrect.

Just keep flying.

Let clarity return on the other side.

The Inner Math

When you're confused or anxious, rash action feels like relief. But *impulsive correction* often creates more deviation.

Especially during:

- ✦ Major transitions
- ✦ Emotional overwhelm
- ✦ New environments
- ✦ High-stakes uncertainty

You can't navigate wisely with scrambled instruments.

Usually, clarity is something you steer toward—like a VOR radial. But occasionally, clarity isn't something you chase. It's a signal you wait for.

This hack trains your restraint. It protects your trajectory.

And it builds your capacity to fly in low visibility without abandoning yourself.

The Vibe to Look For

"I don't know what I'm doing." → Maybe not yet. Stay the course. Let guidance return.

"I need to fix this right now." → Or you need to not make it worse. Don't oversteer.

"I feel lost." → You're not lost. You're in the Cone. And it will pass.

✧ ✧ ✧

Transitions can scramble your signal. But the Cone of Confusion is temporary.

The guidance returns.

The clarity comes back.

And when it does—you'll still be flying true.

Hold your course.

Wait for the needle.

Don't bet the farm in the fog.

✦ ✦ ✦

A conversation with yourself
(or with an Anam Cara)

1. What part of my current life feels most connected to this hack?

2. Was there a season in my past where this tool would have made a difference?

3. Where in my life could applying this tool shake up the status quo?

4. Who do I see who lives this wisdom—or could use it now?

5. Who might enjoy exploring the possibilities of this hack with me?

✦ ✦ ✦

DON'T GET BEHIND THE POWER CURVE

*There's a point where pushing harder
doesn't speed you up.*

The Story Behind the Hack

Every pilot learns about the danger of getting behind the power curve. It's not just an idea—it's a *felt* experience. A moment when the aircraft's energy state drops low enough that even full power can't easily save you.

Behind the power curve, it takes *more* thrust to go *slower* than it does to go faster. That's because of the tricky relationship between lift and drag—especially at low airspeeds.

It's a dangerous place to be.

And once you're there, it takes deliberate, sometimes counterintuitive moves to get out.

Many landings *do* operate behind the power curve. But that's okay—because you're prepared for it.

You've accounted for the drag.

You've configured for this stage.

The danger comes when it happens unexpectedly. When the aircraft slows too much . . . when drag piles on . . . when energy quietly bleeds away and you don't notice in time.

When you've put yourself behind the power curve.

Every seasoned pilot develops a seat-of-the-pants sense of this. That internal *uh-oh* when the aircraft starts to feel mushy. Heavy. Sluggish.

You know: This isn't sustainable. I need to act. Now.

Being behind the power curve in life feels eerily similar. When life feels mushy, sluggish, unresponsive. It's when you're:

+ Working harder and harder . . . but getting less and less return.

+ Pouring in more energy . . . and going slower.

+ Losing momentum . . . but still adding power.

This happens gradually—just like in a jet.

It creeps in through overload, neglect, or denial.

It feels like burnout, overcommitment, or mounting inefficiency.

What Drag Looks Like in Real Life

What causes this drag?

Most of the time, it's self-induced.

Sometimes it's internal. Sometimes it's circumstantial. Sometimes it's accumulated.

But the results are the same: wasted energy and rising vulnerability.

Some of the most common culprits:

- ✦ Poor time management — constantly late, rushed, or unreliable
- ✦ Lack of preparation — walking into meetings, tests, or interviews unready
- ✦ Not listening or learning — refusing to absorb feedback or upskill
- ✦ Overspending — living beyond your means
- ✦ Overpromising — committing beyond your bandwidth

- ✦ Tolerating mistreatment — until exiting requires *everything* you've got
- ✦ Saying yes to everything — until you're underwater
- ✦ Carrying too much emotional weight — without boundaries or support

And then there's the quieter drag:

- ✦ Obligations that no longer match your life
- ✦ Roles you outgrew but never stepped out of
- ✦ Guilt, fear, or unresolved patterns that eat fuel in the background

Sometimes drag is external—like ice building up on the wings, or a bad economy.

Sometimes it's internal—like poor configuration or poor planning.

And sometimes, we're simply flying heavy:

Big dreams. Big responsibilities. Long-haul missions with lots of cargo.

That's not wrong. But when you're heavy, you need:

- ✦ More margin
- ✦ Sharper awareness
- ✦ Quicker detection of energy loss

Or you'll sink below sustainable flight.

How To Use This Tool

This hack is about energetic intelligence—the science of energy management.

Start noticing when you're carrying or creating a lot of drag in your life, when you're nearing the edge of your performance envelope:

- ✦ You're constantly behind. You're constantly exhausted.
- ✦ You're doing more and accomplishing less.
- ✦ You're afraid to stop because *everything* might fall apart.
- ✦ You're one setback away from collapse.

That's your warning: you're behind the power curve. And once you're there, recovery takes more than just effort, more than just willpower.

It takes:

- ✦ Reducing drag
- ✦ Shedding unnecessary load
- ✦ Adjusting your angle of ambition
- ✦ Creating space to regain momentum

The answer is rarely more thrust or more hustle. It's better configuration.

The Inner Math

"Behind the power curve" is just the name of the problem. But power usually isn't the issue—drag is. And drag doesn't always look like clutter.

It can look like:

- ✦ Obligation
- ✦ Poor habits
- ✦ Legacy commitments
- ✦ Complexity
- ✦ Even love—if it's misaligned with your actual life

This hack invites you to fly smarter, not just harder.

It asks:

- ✦ What am I carrying that no longer serves this mission?
- ✦ What am I doing that burns fuel without gaining ground?
- ✦ What configuration would give me back some lift?

The Vibe to Look For

"I just need to try harder." → Or maybe you need to reconfigure.

"Everything is taking too much effort." → You're behind the curve. Look for drag.

"I can't slow down—it'll all fall apart." → That's a stall warning. Start there.

✧ ✧ ✧

You're allowed to carry big dreams.

You're allowed to fly long distances.

But you're not designed to operate at max power just to stay in the air—just to survive.

Fly smart.

Notice drag.

Stay ahead of the power curve.

✧ ✧ ✧

A conversation with yourself
(or with an Anam Cara)

1. What part of my current life feels most connected to this hack?

2. Was there a season in my past where this tool would have made a difference?

3. Where in my life could applying this tool shake up the status quo?

4. Who do I see who lives this wisdom—or could use it now?

5. Who might enjoy exploring the possibilities of this hack with me?

✧ ✧ ✧

FOCUS ON THE
TASK AT HAND

When judgment is loud,
focus is your quiet rebellion.

The Story Behind
the Hack

I'm going to get a little vulnerable here.

Flying is still an overwhelmingly male-dominated field. When I was hired at a major airline, women made up just over 3 percent of airline pilots.

By the time I retired, we had only climbed to about 7 percent. Progress? Technically, yes. But in reality, it meant spending my entire career under a microscope.

Despite my credentials—a former military pilot, with years of operational experience—I felt the pressure of scrutiny every day.

And not just for myself.

The comments about affirmative action. The sideways remarks about DEI. The assumptions. The suggestion that you don't *really* belong.

It was relentless. And it was exhausting. And yes—it was unfair.

The unrelenting scrutiny got under my skin. It hit me physically—tight jaw, stomach aches, fatigue, and a rising tide of performance anxiety.

I was living my dream job. And seriously thinking about quitting.

Not because I wasn't capable.

Not because I wasn't qualified.

But because I was tired of proving it. Tired of flying every leg like it was a courtroom.

For a long time, I was angry. And to be clear—it *was* unfair.

It *is* unfair to expect people from underrepresented groups to prove their competence over and over again—even after checkrides, emergencies, and years as captain—while the dominant group is assumed capable from the start.

But one day, I realized something that shifted everything:

Unfair or not, I was the one suffering. I was the one clenching my jaw. I was the one with the anxiety.

The people making casual, cutting comments? They were sleeping just fine.

So I made a decision: I would take charge of my attention.

How to Use This Tool

Performance anxiety thrives on divided attention. It feeds off the gap between what you're *doing* and what you *fear others are thinking* about what you're doing.

This hack collapses that gap.

Sometimes, agitators are just parroting something they heard online. Sometimes their comments have sharper edges.

They *want* to rattle your confidence.

They *want* you to quit.

I decided that no matter what others said or assumed, I would no longer let them fly my jet—or take up space in my mind. I would focus on what mattered.

And what mattered was this:

The task at hand.

Not their commentary. Not their story about who belongs. Not their fantasy about how I got here.

Just:

- What does this moment require?
- What is the next best step?
- What needs to be done?

Focus on the task at hand. That was the hack.

Over time—and with a lot of practice—it became second nature. And like most good hacks, it worked.

When you do that—*really* do it—it quiets the noise. And over time, it becomes a kind of superpower:

The ability to direct your energy toward what matters, even under pressure.

The Inner Math

Looking back, I realize now: those thoughtless comments were acting like drag on my system. They were slowing me down—not because they were true, but because I was hauling them with me.

I had let them put me behind the power curve. Even

as I flew well, I was burning more fuel than I needed—just to stay aloft.

Focusing on the task at hand meant letting go of that drag.

It meant reclaiming my attention. It meant disentangling from their noise. It meant giving myself the focus they took for granted.

And *that's* when the real freedom began.

The Vibe to Look For

"But what will they think of me?" → Doesn't matter. Focus on what's needed now.

"I don't want to prove them right." → You don't have to. Just fly the jet.

"I feel like I don't belong here." → You *do*. Focus on the task. Let it speak for itself.

✧ ✧ ✧

Clarity is a rebellion. Focus is a refuge.

Let their projections drift away like turbulence. Fly your mission. Own your mind.

Focus on the task at hand.

✧ ✧ ✧

A conversation with yourself
(or with an Anam Cara)

1. What part of my current life feels most connected to this hack?

2. Was there a season in my past where this tool would have made a difference?

3. Where in my life could applying this tool shake up the status quo?

4. Who do I see who lives this wisdom—or could use it now?

5. Who might enjoy exploring the possibilities of this hack with me?

✧ ✧ ✧

improve your position

You don't need certainty to start planning or acting.
You just need vision—and the willingness to begin.

The Story Behind
the Hack

This book took twenty years to write. So did my memoir. So will a couple of other books waiting in the wings.

I had the ideas a long time ago—sometimes clear, sometimes only a whisper. But it wasn't the right season. The clarity hadn't arrived. Or life was full with other responsibilities.

So instead of forcing it . . . I improved my position.

I opened a document. Gave it a working title. And when a line came, or an idea appeared that felt like it belonged—I added it. No pressure. No deadline. Just trust.

I've used this same strategy since middle school— long before I picked up the phrase in the military or the cockpit.

Remodeling a house?

Making a cross-country move?

Launching something that feels too big or too early?

I don't panic.

I improve my position.

Sometimes, life doesn't give you the green light yet. Doesn't even show you the final destination. The opportunity isn't ready. The doors aren't open.

You're not even sure how it could all come together.

That's okay. This isn't a moment for landing the dream. It's a moment to improve your position.

This hack is the cousin to *Tiny Is Terrific*.

But while *Tiny* is about breaking free from paralysis through micro-movement, *Improve Your Position* is about vision—and developing the plans that bring it to life.

In aviation, pilots are trained to stay far ahead of the aircraft. Not just 10 minutes. Often 1–3 hours ahead or more—tracking weather, fuel, delays, alternates, and arrival conditions.

We don't wait until we're on top of a thunderstorm to make a decision.

We think ahead.

We plan the mission—and keep refining it as we go.

Even when we can't act yet, we're asking:

Where are we headed?

What could get in the way?

What needs to happen between now and then?

How to Use This Tool

This hack is for the middle space:

Not quite ready for final push to the finish line . . . but ready to lay groundwork.

It's about doing what you *can* while mapping out what's still unknown.

Ask yourself:

"What would I do if I *did* know how to move forward?"

Then sketch it out.

Get specific.

You don't need to know everything—just the next layer that's within reach.

From there, you can:

- ✦ Create a vision.
- ✦ Draft a plan.
- ✦ Break it into stages.
- ✦ Act on what's already actionable.
- ✦ Research the gaps.
- ✦ Rework the map as clarity unfolds.

Here's what it looks like in real life:

Want to buy a house?

- ✦ You don't need to wait for the perfect market.
- ✦ Create a budget. Research the options. Build a savings plan.
- ✦ Position yourself now—so you're ready when the window opens.

Want to retire early?

- ✦ Do the math.
- ✦ Create a bucket list.
- ✦ What will you do in your free time?
- ✦ Where would you want to live?

Want that coveted internship?

- ✦ You may not know how to get in.
- ✦ But if you did—what would your steps be?
- ✦ Who would you talk to? What would you need on your resume?
- ✦ Start filling in those blanks.

This is the planning most people postpone until *after* the door opens. But by then—it's too late to prepare.

This hack flips that.

You prepare *before* you know exactly how.

You plan forward—using the scaffolding of what's already in reach.

The Inner Math

Everything rests on something else. No success stands alone. No opportunity comes out of thin air.

We don't build the house *after* everything's perfect.

We draw up the plans *before* the land is even bought— and then we redraw the plans to fit the land we find.

If you're waiting until the timing is ideal, the path is clear, or you're "ready" . . . you'll miss it.

This hack helps you build a future that can *meet* the timing when it arrives.

Even if the first draft of your plan is wrong—it's still useful.

Because now you have scaffolding.

Now you can revise.

Now you can recognize the path when it appears.

> *Luck is what happens when preparation meets opportunity.*
> —Attributed to Seneca (and many others)

This is how synchronicity meets strategy.

The Vibe To Look For

"There's nothing I can do right now." → Not true. You can plan. You can prepare. You can position.

"But I don't know how it's going to happen." → You don't need to. Just ask: *If I did know, what might it look like and what actions can I take now?*

"Isn't planning a waste if things change?" → No. Planning isn't prediction. It's preparation.

✧ ✧ ✧

You don't need full clarity to build a foundation.

You don't need permission to draw a blueprint.

Improve your position.

So when the door opens—you're not scrambling.

You're stepping into a future you've already shaped.

✧ ✧ ✧

A CONVERSATION WITH YOURSELF
(or with an Anam Cara)

1. What part of my current life feels most connected to this hack?

2. Was there a season in my past where this tool
   would have made a difference?

3. Where in my life could applying this tool shake
   up the status quo?

4. Who do I see who lives this wisdom—or could
   use it now?

5. Who might enjoy exploring the possibilities of
   this hack with me?

✧ ✧ ✧

PAY THE PRICE—
OR DON'T

Everything costs something.
You don't have to do everything.
But know what you're choosing—and choose it on purpose.

The Story Behind
the Hack

This hack didn't come from aviation. It came from life as an author, a small business owner, and a coach—a life full of experts saying, *"This is what you have to do."*

Build your platform.

Grow your audience.

Post more. Hustle harder.

Follow the funnel.

Master the launch.

Some of it was wise. Some of it even worked. But a lot of it felt energetically expensive—and sometimes financially overwhelming.

It didn't feel aligned. It didn't feel alive. It felt like I was paying a cost . . . just to keep up with others.

In those moments, I could feel myself start to spiral:

I'll get left behind.

Maybe I'm not cut out for this.

If I don't do this, I'll fail.

That's the victim voice.

But then something shifted.

What if I didn't have to do it? What if I simply looked at the price of doing the thing—and the price of not doing the thing—and chose one?

What if I said:

"Yes, this strategy might bring success. But I don't want to pay that price right now. And I'm at peace with that."

Suddenly, I had sovereignty again.

Suddenly, I wasn't drowning—I was deciding.

And sometimes, with time, the whole field changes.

Gatekeepers leave. Technology evolves. The thing that once felt hard becomes simple.

You grow. Your alignment shifts.

But that clarity always remains: You don't have to do everything.

If you do opt out—do it consciously. Know what you're gaining. And what you're letting go.

How To Use This Tool

This hack is for moments of pressure—when a solution is being pushed hard, but it doesn't feel right.

It's for the moments when:

- ✦ You're told you "have to" hustle 24/7 to succeed.
- ✦ You're told to speak up, go public, or stay silent—when none of it feels true to you.
- ✦ You're weighing the cost of doing something scary, or the cost of staying where you are.

In those moments, pause. Ask:

What is the actual price of this path?

What is the price of not taking it?

Am I willing to pay either?

Then choose.

You can pay the price of growth. Or the price of peace.

But when you choose—really choose—there's no resentment. You're no longer a victim of a complicated world.

You're a sovereign person making a clear call.

The Inner Math

This hack reframes success—and failure.

It's not about whether you're willing to do what others are doing. It's about whether you're willing to live with your choice. And not shame yourself for making it— or envy or resent someone else's success.

If you don't want to market your book at the level everyone recommends, that's okay.

If you don't want to open a lawsuit, tell your story publicly, or leave your job today—that's okay too.

Just don't pretend you're powerless. You're not stuck. You're choosing. And you can choose again later.

The Vibe to Look For

"But I'll fall behind if I don't." → Maybe. Are you willing to pay that price? Then choose it.

"I just don't want to." → Okay. Then own it.

"I'm tired of the pressure." → Then free yourself by deciding—clearly.

✧ ✧ ✧

Peace has a price. So does success.

But resentment, confusion, and paralysis? Those are the most expensive of all.

So name the price.

Weigh the cost.

And then:

Pay the price—or don't.

But do it on purpose.

A CONVERSATION WITH YOURSELF
(or with an Anam Cara)

1. What part of my current life feels most connected to this hack?

2. Was there a season in my past where this tool would have made a difference?

3. Where in my life could applying this tool shake up the status quo?

4. Who do I see who lives this wisdom—or could use it now?

5. Who might enjoy exploring the possibilities of this hack with me?

✧ ✧ ✧

PAY YOURSELF FIRST

Abundance begins with intention—
and a quiet decision to honor your future self first.

The Story Behind the Hack

This one didn't come from aviation. But looking back, I realize—it's the antidote to getting behind the power curve. It's also the root system beneath many of the other hacks:

Tiny is Terrific. Improve Your Position. Don't Get Behind the Power Curve.

This one quietly powers them all.

I learned this from a professor at the Air Force Academy—a colonel who became a millionaire on the modest military salary of that time.

He was also unusually generous. He'd often treat his entire class to ice cream. He didn't act like someone hoarding wealth—he modeled peace and abundance with it.

He said something that rewired my mindset forever:

"Pay yourself first."

Instead of waiting to see what was *left* at the end of the month and hoping I'd have enough to save, I followed his advice. I created a budget and decided in advance what to set aside. That went out first. Automatically. And whatever was left, I could spend without guilt or worry.

I had already taken care of my future self. It wasn't deprivation. It was clarity.

It wasn't about scarcity. It was a mindset of enough.

More Than Just Money

This professor gave us other financial wisdom, too:

+ Don't buy the fancy car at graduation.
+ Buy something simple. You've already won.
+ When you get promoted, don't inflate your lifestyle.

- ✦ You've already been living on less.
- ✦ Bank the difference. Let it work for you.

These lessons stuck.

It took me a few years to build the habit—but once I did, it became autopilot. As automatic as paying a mortgage.

No more dread at the end of the month. No more guilt. Just peace. But here's the deeper truth:

This hack isn't just about money.

It's about your energy.

Your time.

Your emotional nourishment.

Your spiritual alignment.

Your mental health.

Paying yourself first means knowing what actually matters—and making sure that thing is tended before the world comes knocking.

How To Use This Tool

This is a hack for long-range peace.

- ✦ Want to be financially stable? Automate your savings—even if it's small.

- ✦ Want to avoid burnout? Build in your recovery time—first, not last.

- ✦ Want to stay in alignment? Schedule the walk. Take the break. Journal. Meditate.

- ✦ Want to write a book? Don't wait for leftover time. Create sacred space at the front end.

Whatever your "wealth" is—treat it like a priority. Don't save your best self for what's left over.

This hack builds a buffer. A margin. A deep habit of sovereignty. Over time, it compounds—like interest. And before you know it, you're living in the future you built on purpose.

The Inner Math

If you wait to invest in yourself until everything else is done—you'll never invest at all.

You'll keep reacting. Keep spending down your reserves. Keep living behind the power curve. But if you flip the equation—just once—it changes everything.

"I matter first."

"My well-being gets a line item."

"I take care of the roots, not just the branches."

And from that place—abundance flows. Not just in your account. But in your spirit.

The Vibe to Look For

"I'll save what's left at the end of the month." → Flip it. Pay yourself first.

"I'll rest when everything's done." → No. Rest is how you stay in the game.

"I feel guilty putting myself first." → It's not selfish. It's sustainable.

✧ ✧ ✧

You are not what's leftover. You are not the thing to be squeezed into the margins. So pay yourself first.

Financially. Emotionally. Energetically. Creatively.

And build a life that honors your deepest values—not just your loudest obligations.

Abundance begins not when you have everything—but when you decide to honor what matters most.

✧ ✧ ✧

A conversation with yourself
(or with an Anam Cara)

1. What part of my current life feels most connected to this hack?

2. Was there a season in my past where this tool would have made a difference?

3. Where in my life could applying this tool shake up the status quo?

4. Who do I see who lives this wisdom—or could use it now?

5. Who might enjoy exploring the possibilities of this hack with me?

✧ ✧ ✧

Curious how others are using these hacks?

Looking for a place to talk this out?

Bring your reflections to The Flying Club Lounge

on Facebook ...

Where growth is the adventure—
and you don't have to do it alone.

Find us here by either scanning the QR code,
or visiting the short link below:

https://bit.ly/TheFlyingClubLounge

THE JOURNEY IS YOURS

If you've made it this far, you've already done something unusual in a noisy, pressured world. You stopped. You've chosen to reflect. To engage. To claim your life as a path worth navigating on purpose.

These hacks weren't handed down as commandments. They're simply tools—field-tested insights from a life in motion:

In the air, on the ground, and in the deep interior of what it means to live with integrity.

Some of them will stick. Some may fade.

As one of my mentors once said: "Take the best, and leave the rest."

But every one was offered with a single hope:

That you will learn to navigate from the wisdom within.

We live in a world of noise, pressure, confusion, and urgency. But beneath it all is something quieter. Steadier. Wiser.

You.

You are the compass.

You are the mapmaker.

You are the one charting the course.

And as every seasoned traveler learns:

There is no perfect route.

Only adjustments.

Only awareness.

Only the willingness to orient—and reorient—toward what's true.

So wherever you are in your journey—

Walk with courage.

Navigate with clarity.

And never forget to pay yourself first.

The journey is yours.

With respect and joy,

Captain Patty

Books by Patty Bear

If you're curious about the journey from Old Order Mennonite
roots to the cockpit of jet aircraft—and the deeper truths
unearthed along the way—check out these titles:

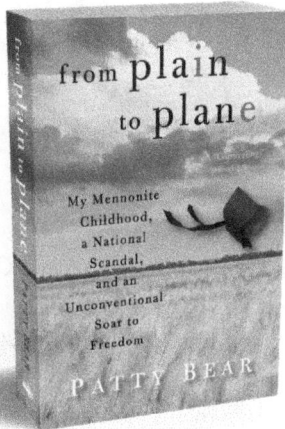

From Plain to Plane:
My Mennonite Childhood, a National Scandal,
and an Unconventional Soar to Freedom

A memoir of awakening, rebellion, and resilience—tracing one
woman's flight from the confines of religious authority, family
loyalty, and cultural conditioning toward an uncompromising
freedom of spirit. The origin story of a soul navigator breaking
free from inherited maps.

Second place winner, IBPA Benjamin Franklin Award 2022

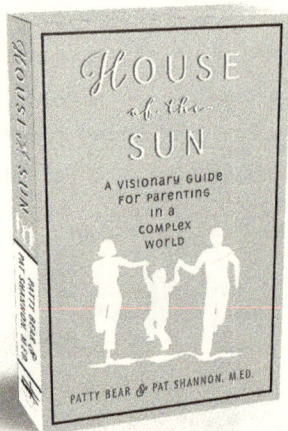

House of the Sun:
A Visionary Guide for Parenting in a Complex World

A visionary and practical guide to raising children with both Warmth and Order—the two foundational forces every child needs to thrive. More than a parenting book, it's a compass for showing up with presence, emotional maturity, and inner wisdom—especially when the world feels complex or overwhelming.

Co-written with an early childhood expert, this book helps you grow alongside your children, offering grounded insights for parenting with clarity, connection, and confidence.

Together with *Captain Patty's Wisdom Hacks*, it's part of a growing collection of tools for navigating life with soul, discernment, and self-leadership.

.

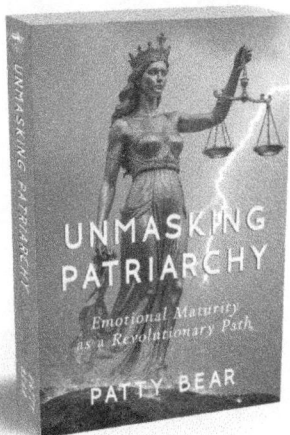

Unmasking Patriarchy:
Claiming Emotional Maturity as a Revolutionary Path
(Coming November 2025 – Available for preorder)

A fierce and lucid exploration of the hidden psychological terrain we all navigate. *Unmasking Patriarchy* maps the emotional immaturity at the heart of systems that shape our choices, identities, roles, and relationships—from family systems and faith structures to political and cultural power.

This is not a book about men versus women. It's about the ancient architecture of immaturity in the seat of power we've all been shaped by—and the clarity we need to rise beyond it.

Offering both map and compass, this book equips readers with the tools to navigate this terrain with greater agility, self-leadership, and freedom—personally and collectively.

ACKNOWLEDGMENTS

This book is rooted in lived experience—and I've been graced with many teachers along the way.

To all the wise souls who've shared their insights, offered their stories, or simply lived with such presence that I took quiet notes—thank you.

To my children, Morgan and Evan—both born old souls. You've taught me more than you probably know.

To my husband, Kevin, who occasionally drops a sentence so crisp and true I have to stop what I'm doing and write it down.

To my Anam Caras and wisdom carriers—Pat, Monica, Gretchen, Mary, Lynn, Sally, Liz, Deb, Aspen, Martie, Glenna, Michael, Hadley, Stacey, Kathy—and so many others who've walked beside me, held space, and told the truth.

To the mentors, colleagues, and role models who embodied excellence in a variety of ways—sometimes without even realizing it. Some of your names I've forgotten, but your influence remains. Others I'll name with gratitude here: Bebe, Joe C. (RIP), Dave P., Phil M. (RIP), Pat Shannon, Heather, Gene K., Diane E., Ken F., Kathleen H., Julie H., Cathy J., Linda R.

To the tradespeople and craftspeople I've met over the years —your attention to detail and pride in your work quietly shaped my own sense of standards and care.

To my new village neighbors—thank you for reminding me that community still matters, and that kindness is a form of quiet brilliance.

And of course, this is just a partial list. I've surely forgotten more names than I've remembered. Please forgive me if yours is one of them.

To the negative role models, too—a sincere bow. Sometimes the clearest guidance comes from witnessing what not to do. You helped me grow by contrast. I couldn't have charted my own path without you either.

To all of you—named and unnamed—thank you for being part of this adventure.

Finally, I must acknowledge my brilliant editor, book designer, and wise woman who has also become a dear friend: Stacey Aaronson. I wouldn't trust anyone else with my books. She has an uncanny ability to tune into my work as if she were me—fine-tuning in my voice, and intuiting what a book needs before I've even imagined it. And I know I'm not alone; she brings this same gift to every author she works with. Her attention to detail is legendary, her commitment to professionalism and excellence unflagging. Beyond all that, she models kindness, strong boundaries, deep wisdom, and the kind of infectious laughter and encouragement that lights the creative path and nourishes the soul.

aBOUT THE auTHor

PATTY BEAR is a retired airline captain, raised Old Order Mennonite, and award-winning author. She writes for adventurers of growth—badass souls, misfits, mystics, truth seekers, and anyone longing to live more vividly. The ones who question old patterns, walk new paths, and bravely step into the life they were born to live. Her work distills complexity and inherited scripts into clarity, direction, self-leadership, and freedom.

She is the author of *House of the Sun: A Visionary Guide for Parenting in a Complex World* and the award-winning memoir *From Plain to Plane: My Mennonite Childhood, a National Scandal, and an Unconventional Soar to Freedom*.

www.theflyingclub.com

Would You Leave a Quick Review, Please?
It Helps More Than You Know.

If this book gave you a new lens, a gut-check, or a sentence that stuck with you—I'd love to hear about it.

You don't have to write a novel. Just a few honest lines on Amazon, Goodreads, or wherever you hang out online helps more than you think.

Here's an easy way to frame it:

+ Which hack hit home for you—and why?
+ Which one made you go "Darn, I wish I had this sooner"?
+ Who would you hand this book to right now?

Whether it made you laugh, think deeper, or plot your next big move . . . your voice helps this book find its people.

Thanks for showing up. And thanks for sharing what's real.

— Captain Patty

www.ingramcontent.com/pod-product-compliance
Lightning Source LLC
Chambersburg PA
CBHW031929090426
42811CB00002B/125